Col. William B. Travis

The Alamo

TEXAS

Yesterday and Today

By

Sibyl Hancock
and
Fay Venable

EAKIN PRESS   ★   AUSTIN, TEXAS

For Julie Tordaro

TABLE OF CONTENTS

SAM HOUSTON
First President of the Republic of Texas

I. HISTORY

"Get ready!" Davy Crockett shouted. "Here they come!"

The men in the old mission called the Alamo aimed their guns. They watched as lines of Mexican soldiers marched toward them. The Texans had battled Mexico for thirteen days. They were fighting to free Texas from Mexican rule.

Mexico's laws governing Texas were harsh and unfair. On March 2, 1836. Texas had declared its independence as a republic.

On March 6 the Mexicans led by Mexico's General Santa Anna attacked the Texans in the Alamo.

There were only 157 men in the Alamo. There were at least four or five thousand Mexican soldiers surrounding them. The Texans had held back the Mexican army as long as they could.

"Fire!" Davy Crockett yelled.

Many of the Mexicans fell as bullets struck them. But others took their places. Mexican soldiers reached the Alamo and began climbing its walls. The Texans fought bravely, even though they knew they could not win.

When the battle was over, not one Texas soldier in the Alamo was alive. The deaths of the men at the Alamo made the people of Texas very angry. "Remember the Alamo!" became a battle cry.

While the battle at the Alamo was going on, General Sam Houston was gathering another army of Texans to fight the Mexicans. On April 21, 1836,

Statue of Sam Houston in Houston, Texas

General Houston led the attack of the Battle of San Jacinto. He surprised the Mexicans during their siesta or nap time. Many Mexican soldiers were so frightened they jumped into the San Jacinto River and drowned.

General Santa Anna tried to get away, but he was caught. Santa Anna was the dictator of Mexico. His great army had been defeated by a small band of Texans. At Sam Houston's order, Santa Anna signed a paper declaring Texas forever free from Mexico.

Texas was a republic for nine years. On December 29, 1845, Texas became the twenty-eighth state to join the United States. The Texas Republic flag bearing one star became the state flag. Texas is known as the Lone Star State.

2

Spanish Soldiers In Texas

Indians were the first Texans.

Early History

Indians lived in Texas long before white men or Mexicans. The Caddo tribe was peaceful. Its people were gentle and intelligent. The Apache and Comanche tribes of West Texas were fierce and warlike. In years to come they would fight many battles with settlers who began moving onto the rich land.

In 1598 a young man, Don Juan de Onate, rode across the Rio Grande River from Mexico into Texas. He claimed Texas as a possession of Spain in the name of the king of Spain.

Texas stayed under Spanish rule for many years. In 1821 Mexico won independence from Spain. Texas then belonged to the Mexican Republic.

In that same year Stephen F. Austin started a colony of Americans in Texas. The Mexican government granted Austin land for his settlers. He brought 300 families to make their homes along the Brazos River. Soon many settlers began to come to Texas.

Throughout its history, the flags of six nations have flown over Texas. These nations were Spain, France, Mexico, the Republic of Texas, the Confederate States of America, and the United States. Texas got its name from the Indian word "tejas" meaning "friends."

A Real Indian Princess
Daughter of Chief Quanah Parker

5

II. GEOGRAPHY

Cathedral Room in Cascade Cavern

Photo courtesy of Cascade Caverns

Today there are about 13 million people living in Texas. This great state lies in the southwestern part of the United States. It is the second largest state in the Union. It is 800 miles across from north to south and east to west.

Most of Texas is a huge plain. The land is 4,000 feet high in northwest Texas. It slopes southward to sea level as it meets the Gulf of Mexico.

Texas has many different kinds of countryside. There are tall mountains and level plateaus. There are bright canyons and dark caves. Flat farm and ranch land and thick woods fill millions of Texas' acres.

Thousands of shining lakes are dotted around Texas. Some of these lakes were made by men. Texas also has many rivers. Most of them flow south and empty into the Gulf of Mexico.

Terraced farm land   Circular sprinkler systems irrigate farm land

Texas can be divided into four areas. These are the Coastal Plains, the Central Plains, the High Plains, and the Western Mountain Region.

In the southern part of the Coastal Plains is the fertile Rio Grande River Valley. It is famous for its winter fruits and vegetables. People all over the country eat Texas grapefruit, oranges, lemons, and limes. Other favorites are tomatoes, potatoes, cantelopes, and watermelons.

The East Texas oil field is also located in the Coastal Plains area. It is one of the largest oil fields in the world. Texas produces a fourth of the nation's oil.

Huge forests grow in the Coastal Plains. Most of the trees are pine. There are also oak, gum, pecan, cypress, and many others. The center of the Texas lumber business is located here.

The Central Plains has many valleys, canyons, caves, and hills. The rolling hills are located on the western edge of the Central Plains. This is sometimes called the Hill Country. There are fields of cotton and grain. There are also deposits of coal, gas, oil, salt, and sulfur in this area.

Oil wells near Baytown, Texas

East Texas pine trees

The High Plains is made up of vast stretches of flat land. It has very few shrubs or large trees. Mesquite trees and cactus grow on this plain. The Texas Panhandle is found in the north part of this region. Cotton and wheat grow well here. Texas has more farms than any other state. And there are many large cattle ranches. There are oil fields in the High Plains area.

The Western Mountain Region is in the far western part of Texas. The state's mountains rise out of the sandy land. The highest point is Guadalupe Mountain. It is 8,751 feet high. The land is mainly used for ranching. It is rocky and dry. Ranchers have windmills that pump water into ponds and tanks for their cattle.

III. WEATHER

Weather in Texas can change suddenly. In the spring there are quick thunderstorms with high winds and heavy rains. Sandstorms are blown by winds in West Texas. Sometimes in the fall a hurricane sweeps onto the coast from the Gulf of Mexico. These violent storms can cause great damage to the port cities and towns.

It may be hot in South Texas and freezing in North Texas at the same time. Thousands of people go to South Texas to spend the winters. They usually live in their travel trailers. These people are nicknamed "snowbirds."

The soil in Texas is sandy on the plains. There is black clay in the eastern region. The soil is rich along the river banks.

9

Damage made by hurricane.

High winds of hurricane striking land.

Exxon Refinery

IV. INDUSTRY

More cotton and rice is grown in Texas than in any other state. There are also fields of wheat, rye, and corn.

Paper mills and lumber yards can be found in the woods of East Texas. Huge trucks travel the roads daily taking logs to the mills.

Cattle raising is one of Texas' largest industries. Sheep are also important to Texas. More wool is produced in Texas than in any other state.

11

STEEL

MADE

IN

TEXAS

AT

BAYTOWN

Harvesting Wheat

Corn field

Watering the farm land

Hay in stacks

Texas is known for its wildlife. Deer, quail, dove, and wild turkey can be found on the western plains and in the East Texas woods.

Texas is one of the world's largest storehouses for crude oil. There are 40 refineries in the state. The largest refinery in the United States is in Texas. There are also great sulfur, salt, and coal deposits. Some of the stone deposits are granite, limestone, asphalt, and mercury.

13

Windmill on cattle ranch

Cowboys Rounding up Texas cattle.

14

V. SOME TEXAS CITIES

"Largest to Smallest"

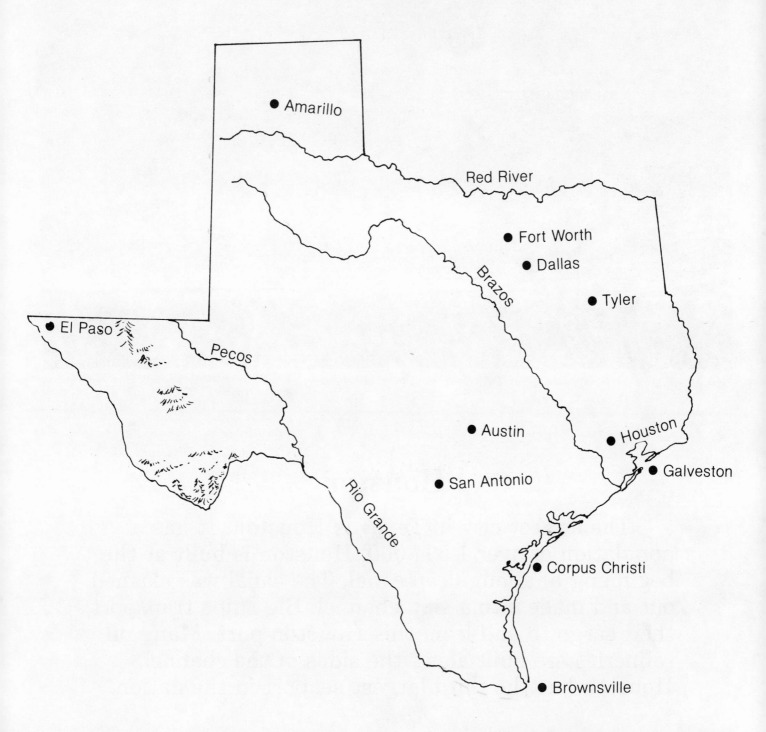

Houston

The largest city in Texas is Houston. It has a population of over 1,594,000. Houston is built at the beginning of a long deep canal. The canal was cleaned out and made into a ship channel. Big ships transport their cargo to and from this Houston port. Many oil refineries are built along the sides of the channel. Houston has the third largest seaport in the nation.

The Astrodome in Houston.

The world famous Astrodome is in Houston. It is one of the largest air-conditioned stadiums in the world. Visitors can see baseball and football games. They can also watch rodeos, motorcycle races, and bullfights there.

Next to the Astrodome is Astroworld. It is a sixty-acre playground filled with exciting rides and entertainment.

Houston Oilers football team

The University of Houston is one of nine colleges in Houston. Many medical students attend classes at the Texas Medical Center. The center is one of the finest in the world.

The San Jacinto Monument is near Houston. It is built on the battleground where Sam Houston defeated Santa Anna in 1836. The monument is the tallest in the world.

The Johnson Spacecraft Center is on the outskirts of Houston. It is the headquarters for America's space program. The astronauts are trained at this center. People can tour the center during visiting hours.

Turning basin at Port of Houston

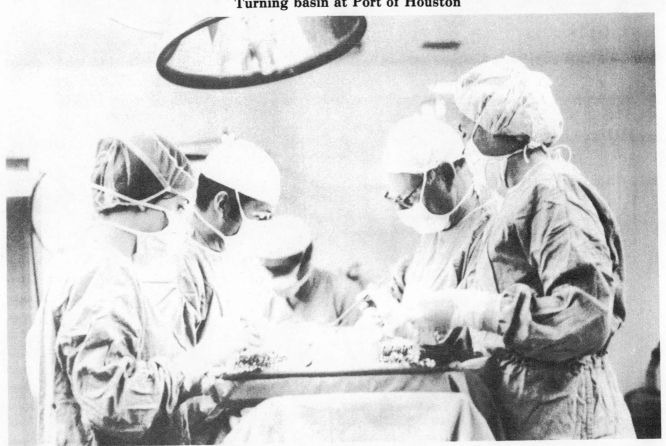

Doctors at work in Houston medical center.

19

Ice Rink at Galleria Shopping Center in Houston **San Jacinto Monument**

Lyndon B. Johnson Space Center—NASA

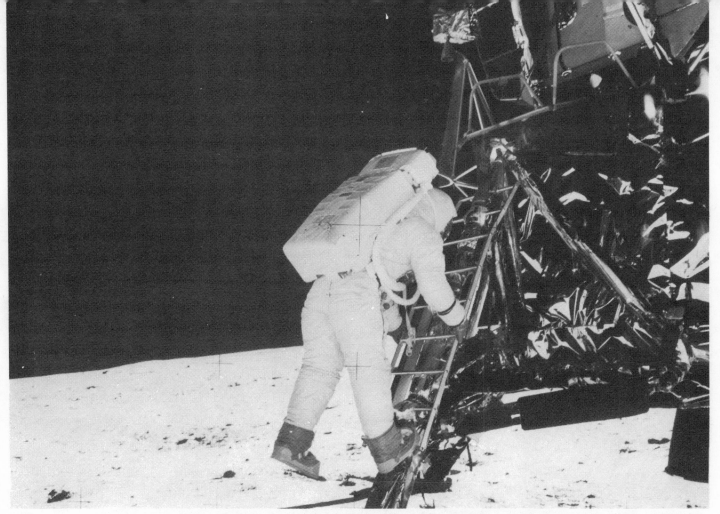

Astronaut steps onto moon.

Photo courtesy of Lyndon B. Johnson Space Center NASA

Astronaut leaves footprint on moon.

21

Dallas

Dallas is in the Central Plains area. With a population of over 900,000, it is the second largest city in Texas. Dallas is a city of art and culture. There are always many good plays and fine paintings to enjoy there. Southern Methodist University is located in the city.

Dallas is the largest banking center in the Southwest. It has more insurance companies than any city in the nation. It is also known as a great shipping center. There are nine main-line railroads and many good highways and airlines for transportation.

State Fair of Texas

Cotton Bowl Stadium   Photo courtesy of State Fair of Texas

23

People at the fair.

There are many ways to have fun while visiting Dallas. The State Fair of Texas has over three million visitors each year. The Cotton Bowl Stadium is on the fair grounds.

The Texas Safari and Game Farm is also a place well worth visiting. People can stay in their cars and watch wild animals walk around the grounds. Sometimes monkeys hop on top of the cars. There are six miles of trails to drive through in this game farm. There are herds of zebra, ostrich, deer, buffalo, antelope, and elk. There are also lions and elephants.

24

San Jose Mission

San Antonio

San Antonio can be found in the Texas Hill Country about 65 miles south of Austin. Over 785,000 people live in the city. They are a mixture of Spanish, Mexican, and Anglo-American.

San Antonio is an old military center. Kelly Air Force Base is the nation's oldest military airfield. There are four air force bases in San Antonio.

There are five Spanish missions in San Antonio. The Alamo is the most famous. It is known as "The Cradle of

Downtown River Walk in San Antonio.

Sunken Garden in a San Antonio park

Texas Liberty." It is in the center of San Antonio. The missions were built in 1718.

The shallow Paseo del Rio winds through the heart of the city. There is a wide walk on each side of the river. Colorful sidewalk cafes and gift shops are built on the river walk. Visitors often ride flat-bottom boats up and down the smooth river.

27

Log cabin village in Fort Worth.

Fort Worth

Fort Worth lies 35 miles west of Dallas. The two cities are so close together, they are called "The Metroplex." Fort Worth has a population of over 385,000. The city has often been called "cow town" by other Texans. After the railroad tracks were laid in Texas,

Fort Worth's "Casa Manana"

Photo courtesy of Fort Worth Chamber of Commerce

cattle were loaded into rail cars in Fort Worth. The city is fast-growing. Texas Christian University is in Fort Worth.

"Six Flags Over Texas" is a great amusement park located near Fort Worth. The theme of the park is based on Texas history.

Having fun at Six Flags Over Texas

Indian Cliffs Ranch near El Paso.

El Paso

El Paso is in the far western corner of Texas. It is called "The City of Sun" because there is very little rainfall. The Rio Grande River flows alongside El Paso. It is here that Texas touches the borders of New Mexico and Mexico. Just across the Rio Grande lies the Mexican city of Juarez. Together, Juarez and El Paso form the largest populated area on the Mexican border. Over 425,000 people live in El Paso.

EL CAPITAN in the Guadalupe Mountains

Photo courtesy of El Paso Convention and Visitor Bureau

In the mountains around El Paso there is a winding scenic drive. A beautiful view of the city can be seen from the mountain drive.

On top of Mt. Cristo Rey, a huge statue of "Christ of the Rockies" stands with arms reaching outward. The statue represents hope for worldwide peace.

Fort Bliss is an army base in El Paso. For many years soldiers have been trained at this base for foreign service.

El Paso has many industries including oil refineries, cotton gins, and stockyards.

Big Bend National Park

To the southeast of El Paso the Rio Grande River makes a great bend. The Big Bend National Park lies inside this curve of the river. And that is how the park got its name.

The park covers 707,895 acres. The land in the park is rough and rugged. The Chisos Mountains rise nearly a mile above the Rio Grande River. *Chisos* is the Spanish word for ghost.

There is a lodge in the park for visitors. People can go on trail rides on horses that are kept in the park. There are also hiking parties to enjoy. The Park Rangers give slide programs each evening. They offer much information about the area.

Austin

Photo courtesy of Austin Chamber of Commerce

Austin is the capitol of Texas and is built on the banks of the Colorado River. The city has a population of over 345,000 people. Austin is in the central part of Texas.

The Capitol building is the largest state capitol in the United States. The building is made of pink granite. The granite came from a Texas rock quarry.

Austin is the home of the University of Texas. And there are five other colleges in the city.

There are large pecan and oak trees in Austin. These old trees add to the beauty of hundreds of picnic areas.

Of the libraries and museums in Austin, the one most visited is the Lyndon B. Johnson Presidential Library. This library has all of former President Johnson's important papers from his many years of public service. A room in the building has been made to look just like the oval room he used as an office in the White House.

Texas State Capitol building

Governor's Mansion

University of Texas Tower

Swimming at the Beach.

Corpus Christi

Corpus Christi is known by its more than 231,000 people as a "shining city by the sea." It is in an area along the Gulf coast called "The Coastal Bend." It is a popular seaport. A twenty-one mile channel connects the city with the Gulf of Mexico.

Padre Island

Padre Island lies across the John F. Kennedy bridge from Corpus Christi. The island is 110 miles long and four miles wide in some places. Padre Island is sometimes called a sand bar. Some of the sand dunes on the island are 50 feet high. Birdwatchers come to the island to see brown pelicans, snow egrets, blue herons, and many others.

Can you catch a Sea Gull?

Amarillo

Amarillo lies in the Texas Panhandle which is the most northern part of Texas. It has been described as "A Young City Going Places." More than 149,000 people live in Amarillo. The land is flat like the top of a table. That is why it is called tableland. Very few trees and shrubs grow in this area.

Amarillo is a great agriculture center. It is surrounded by wheat fields and pasture lands. There are also oil fields and cattle ranches in this plains country.

Longhorn steer

Cattle grazing on a Texas ranch.

41

Palo Duro Canyon

Many years ago cowboys herded longhorn cattle on great cattle drives. They led the cattle on trails that began in the Panhandle and usually ended in Kansas. The railroads had not yet reached Texas. The cattle had to be loaded into rail cars in Kansas and transported to northern cities. Although there are no more trail drives, the cowboy's work is still important in Texas.

The Palo Duro Canyon State Park is near Amarillo. The flat land suddenly drops into an orange and gold canyon. The canyon is more than 1,000 feet deep. Some visitors enjoy camping among the juniper, mesquite, and cottonwood trees growing in the canyon.

Gathering fruit on citrus farm

Brownsville

Brownsville is in the Rio Grande Valley. It is at the southern tip of Texas and lies just across the Rio Grande River from Mexico. Tourists often cross the border to visit the Mexican town of Matamoros. Brownsville is one of the oldest cities in Texas. It was founded in 1846 and was first known as Fort Brown. It has a population of over 84,000.

Brownsville is rich with citrus trees. Workers pick huge loads of grapefruit, oranges, tangerines, and lemons every year.

Rose garden at Tyler

Tyler

Tyler is located in the East Texas oil fields. It is a business town as well as an oil town. It has a population of over 70,000. Although Tyler is not a large city, there are business offices for more than 300 different companies.

Tyler is also known as "The Rose Capitol of the World." A huge rose garden covers 28 acres of land. There are more than 400 kind of roses grown there. Half of the field-grown rose bushes sold in the United States come from Tyler rose gardens.

Indians from the Alabama-Coushatta tribe

The Alabama-Coushatta Indian reservation is in the East Texas woods. There are 4351 acres within the reservation. The Indian village has tribal dances and tours through the village and woods. There is a museum with Indian handwork, art, and jewelry. An outdoor theatre is used by Indian actors to tell the story of their tribe. The play is performed during the summer months.

Galveston

The city of Galveston is on an island in the Gulf of Mexico. It lies one mile from the Texas mainland. There are thirty-two miles of wide sandy beaches on the island. Thousands of visitors come each year to enjoy swimming, fishing, and sunbathing.

This city of over 61,000 people is one of the oldest in Texas. People can visit many fine old homes and see the furnishings in them. Galveston is also an important port city.

Jean Lafitte, the pirate, once lived on Galveston Island. Stories have been told about Lafitte burying his gold and treasures there.

Texans are rugged in spirit. Many of them are descendants of pioneers who came to the big state in covered wagons. Texans are proud of their state's history. They enjoy their mountains, deserts, and beaches. And visitors are always welcome.

46

Old buildings in Galveston

Propoises at Sea-Arama in Galveston

TEXAS FACT PAGE

POPULATION . . . . . . About 13 million people

TOTAL SQUARE MILES 262,134

STATE CAPITOL . . . . Austin

STATE BIRD . . . . Mockingbird

STATE FLOWER . . . . Bluebonnet

STATE TREE . . . . Pecan

STATE MOTTO . . . . Friendship

STATE FLAG . . . . Lone Star

PRESIDENTS   Former Presidents Dwight D.
Eisenhower and Lyndon B. Johnson were
both born in Texas.

STATE SONG . . . . "Texas Our Texas"

STATE FLAG

MOCKING BIRD

PECAN TREE

BLUEBONNET

ABOUT THE AUTHORS

SIBYL HANCOCK

Sibyl Hancock began writing when she was a little girl. She wrote stories about her pets, her family, and her friends. She loved Nancy Drew mysteries and used to wonder what it would be like to be an author like Carolyn Keene, the author of the Nancy Drew books.

In high school Ms. Hancock joined a creative writing club, and one of her poems was published in a national anthology of high school poetry. She attended Sam Houston State University and the University of Houston where she majored in English.

Sibyl Hancock has written numerous reviews of children's books for *The Houston Chronicle*. Ms. Hancock also enjoys her monthly appearances on the CALENDAR program, KHTV-Channel 39 in Houston, where she reviews children's books.

Ms. Hancock has spoken to numerous writers' groups and has participated in teaching seminars. She is listed in *Contemporary Authors* and *Something About The Author*.

Collecting old children's books is one of Ms. Hancock's hobbies. She and her young son, Kevin, have fun adding to their coin collection. She is married to Tom Hancock, a public school administrator.

Her most recent book *Old Blue*, published by Putnam, has been nominated for the prestigious Bluebonnet Award.

FAY VENABLE

Fay Venable, who makes her home in Baytown, has written and had published more than one hundred articles and stories for juvenile and adult publications. Her writings have appeared in *Ranger Rick's Nature Magazine*, *Young World*, *Highlights for Children*, *Jack and Jill*, *Catholic Youth*, *Rock Hound*, *Lapidary Journal*, *Profitable Hobbies* and many others.

She attended Abilene Christian College and the University of Houston where she majored in elementary education. She taught school for ten years and served as librarian for Lee College for ten years. She and her husband are "rockhounds" and have travelled over the state seeking colorful rocks and fossils. She is a member of Associated Authors of Children's Literature, Houston Writer's Workshop, Texas Press Women and the National Federation of Press Women.